49.95

Teen
Safety
Workbook

Facilitator Reproducible
Self-Assessments, Exercises
& Educational Handouts

John J. Liptak, EdD
& Ester R. A. Leutenberg

Illustrated by
Amy L. Brodsky, LISW-S

whole person
Stress & Wellness Publishers
Duluth, Minnesota

Whole Person
210 West Michigan Street
Duluth, MN 55802-1908

800-247-6789

books@wholeperson.com
www.wholeperson.com

Teen Safety Workbook
Facilitator Reproducible Self-Assessments,
Exercises & Educational Handouts

Printed in the United States of America

10 9 8 7 6 5 4 3 2 1

Editorial Director: Carlene Sippola
Art Director: Joy Morgan Dey

Library of Congress Control Number: 2012936857
ISBN: 978-1-57025-264-8

Using This Book *(For the professional)*

Being a teen has always been challenging, but today teens face issues that have been compounded by a rapidly changing society and a plethora of technology. These changes require new strategies in ways to teach teens to protect themselves from the challenges they will constantly face in school and community, and with their friends and family.

Some of the areas in which teens need to worry about their personal safety include:

- Risks related to violence including bullying, exposure to gangs, and harm from guns and other weapons.

- Online dangers including harassment, cyber-bullying, sexually explicit materials, identity theft and financial theft and scams, and agreeing to meet strangers in person after developing online relationships.

- Victimization of crimes.

- Risks while driving in dangerous ways, including driving after drinking or taking drugs, underestimating dangerous road situations, texting or using cell phones inappropriately and not wearing seat belts.

- Putting themselves in personal danger by pressures to do things they do not want to do such as experimenting with drugs and alcohol, having unprotected sex, going to unsafe places by themselves and engaging in risky behaviors.

For teens, staying safe is a much more difficult task than in the past. To help teens sharpen their awareness of the need and ways to stay safe, the *Teen Safety Workbook* will guide them as they explore situations fraught with danger and face people who may threaten their safety.

During adolescence, teens are eager to press to become more independent from their parents, caregivers or family. They need to learn to be more responsible for their own safety. Regardless of whether they are at home, school, work, or in the community, or online, they must face great safety hazards and need to be aware of them. Teen's judgment levels are still forming; most are not ready to make adult level decisions. It is vital for teens to learn that they have the power to keep themselves safe and to be equipped with the tools to overcome dangerous situations.

The *Teen Safety Workbook* is designed to help teens engage in self-reflection, examine their thoughts and feelings that go into the decisions they make, and learn effective tools and techniques to stay safe in the future. This book combines two powerful psychological tools for the management of unsafe, potentially dangerous thoughts, feelings, and behaviors: self-assessment and journaling.

Enrichment activities at the end of each chapter are a third tool for facilitators of teens from families struggling with substance abuse.

(Continued on the next page)

Using This Book *(For the professional, continued)*

The *Teen Safety Workbook* contains five separate sections to help the participants learn more about the choices they have made and the choices they have yet to make in their lives:

Positive Feelings Scale helps teens explore the negative feelings they are experiencing in life and learn effective methods to constructively expressing their emotions.

> *Scale and activities include stress, anger, low self-esteem, depression.*

Healthy Choices Scale helps teens explore how healthy or unhealthy their lifestyle choices are.

> *Scale includes driving, drugs, alcohol and personal safety. Activities include past safe and unsafe choices, a logical decision-making process, a staying safe pledge, warning signs of drug abuse, facts about drinking.*

Social Media Safety Scale helps teens explore safe behaviors while texting, chatting, using social media sites, and surfing the Internet.

> *Scale includes chatting, instant messaging, social media, identity theft, surfing and sexting, etc.*

> *Activities include benefits and negatives of the information highway, online risks, online predators, social media safety, I Wills and Nevers for staying safe online.*

Relationship Safety Scale helps teens explore the safety in their family, friendships, and dating relationships.

> *Scale includes people I'm dating, people at home/in family, friends, neighbor/co-worker, etc. Activities include dating relationship safety, relationships and sexual safety, family/people at home safety, and friend relationship safety; personal safe and unsafe relationships; quotes to consider and journaling prompts; types of abuse; and a safety plan.*

Self-Harm Scale helps teens explore the extent to which they deliberately harm themselves in attempts to cope with intense, overwhelming emotions.

> *Activities include the person's feelings and emotional pain, reasons the person is acting in certain ways, a conscious search for patterns, awareness of anxious energy, stress management techniques, talk about harming oneself, professional treatment, reasons people self-harm.*

Interactive Suggestions for Teens from Families Struggling with Substance Abuse

Teens love to interact with peers. The following options encourage safety-focused thinking, decision-making and behavior, and allow participants to incorporate real life challenges in discussions of these activities: Self Harm Alternatives, Relationships, Positive Feelings, Healthy Choices and Social Media.

At the end of each chapter, following the educational handouts, is a special section for teens from families struggling with substance abuse. The roles teens take in dysfunctional families may lead to unsafe behavior. Teens are encouraged to break the cycle and make healthy and safe changes.

Use Codes for Confidentiality

Confidentiality is a term for any action that preserves the privacy of other people. Because teens completing the activities in this workbook might be asked to answer assessment items and to journal about and explore their relationships, you will need to discuss confidentiality before they begin using the materials in this workbook. Maintaining confidentiality is important as it shows respect for others and allows participants to explore their feelings without hurting anyone's feelings or fearing gossip, harm or retribution.

In order to maintain confidentiality, explain to the participants that they need to assign a name code for each person they write about as they complete the various activities in the workbook. For example, a friend named Joey who enjoys going to hockey games might be titled JLHG (Joey Loves Hockey Games) for a particular exercise. In order to protect all identities, they should not use people's actual names or initials; they must use name codes.

Mandated Reporting Laws

To be aware of the mandated reporting laws, review the website below:

http://www.childwelfare.gov/systemwide/laws_policies/statutes/manda.cfm

Layout of the Book

The *Teen Safety Workbook* is designed to be used either independently or as part of an integrated curriculum. You may administer one of the assessments and the journaling exercises to an individual or a group with whom you are working, or you may administer a number of the assessments over one or more days.

Reproducible Pages:

Assessment Instruments – Self-assessment inventories with scoring directions and interpretation materials. Group facilitators can choose one or more of the activities relevant to their participants.

❑ **Activity Handouts** — Practical questions and activities that prompt self-reflection and promote self-understanding. These questions and activities foster introspection and promote pro-social behaviors.

❑ **Quotations** — Quotations are used in each section to provide insight and promote reflection. Participants will be asked to select one or more of the quotations and journal about what the quotations mean to them.

❑ **Reflective Questions for Journaling** — Self-exploration activities and journaling exercises specific to each assessment to enhance self-discovery, learning, and healing.

❑ **Educational Handouts** — Handouts designed to enhance instruction can be used individually or in groups to promote a positive responsibility for safety at home, in the classroom, and in the community. They can be distributed, scanned and converted into masters for overheads or transparencies, projected or written on boards and/or discussed.

❑ **Enrichment Activities** — A special section at the end of each chapter for teens from families struggling with substance abuse.

Who Should Use This Program?

This book has been designed as a practical tool for helping professionals, such as therapists, school counselors, psychologists, teachers, group leaders, etc. Depending on the role of the professional using the *Teen Safety Workbook* and the specific group's needs, these sections can be used individually or combined for a more comprehensive approach.

Why Use Self-Assessments?

Self-assessments are important in responding to various teen safety issues because they help participants to engage in these ways:

- Become aware of the primary motivators that guide their behavior
- Explore and learn to "let go" of troublesome habits and behavioral patterns
- Explore the effects of unconscious childhood messages
- Gain insight and "a wake-up call" for behavioral change
- Focus their thinking on behavioral goals for change
- Uncover resources they possess that can help them to cope better with safety
- Explore their personal characteristics without judgment
- Recognize and accept their strengths and weaknesses

Because the assessments are presented in a straightforward and easy-to-use format, individuals can self-administer, score and interpret each assessment at their own pace.

About the Assessments, Journaling Activities and Educational Handouts

Materials in the Assessments, Journaling Activities, and Educational Handouts sections in this book are reproducible and can be photocopied for participants' use. Assessments contained in this book focus on self-reported data and thus are similar to ones used by psychologists, counselors, therapists and career consultants. The accuracy and usefulness of the information provided is dependent on the truthful information that each participant provides. By being honest, participants help themselves to learn about unproductive and ineffective patterns in their lives, and to uncover information that might be keeping them from being as happy or as successful as they might be.

An assessment instrument can provide participants with valuable information about themselves; however, these assessments cannot measure or identify everything. The assessments' purpose is not to pigeonhole certain characteristics, but rather to allow participants to explore all of their characteristics. **This book contains self-assessments, not tests.** Tests measure knowledge or whether something is right or wrong. For the assessments in this book, there are no right or wrong answers. These assessments ask for personal opinions or attitudes about a topic of importance in the participant's life.

When administering the assessments in this workbook, remember that the items are generically written so that they will be applicable to a wide variety of people but will not account for every possible variable for every person. No assessments are specifically tailored to one person, so use the assessments to help participants identify negative themes in their lives and find ways to break the hold of these patterns and their effects.

Advise teen participants taking the assessments that they should not spend too much time trying to analyze the content of the questions; they should think about the questions in general and then spontaneously report how they feel about each one. Whatever the results of the assessment, encourage participants to talk about their findings and their feelings pertaining to what have they discovered about themselves. Talking about issues such as aggression and bullying can be therapeutic and beneficial.

The *Teen Safety Workbook* sections serve as an avenue for individual self-reflection, as well as group experiences revolving around identified topics of importance. Each assessment includes directions for easy administration, scoring and interpretation. In addition, each section includes exploratory activities, reflective journaling activities, insightful quotations and educational handouts to help participants to learn more about the ways they put themselves in danger, and to learn more effective skills for being responsible for, and assuring, their personal safety.

(Continued on the next page)

About the Assessments, Journaling Activities and Educational Handouts *(Continued)*

The art of self-reflection goes back many centuries and is rooted in many of the world's greatest spiritual and philosophical traditions. Socrates, the ancient Greek philosopher, was known to walk the streets engaging the people he met in philosophical reflection and dialogue. He felt that this type of activity was so important in life that he proclaimed, "The unexamined life is not worth living!" The unexamined life is one in which the same routine is continually repeated without ever thinking about its meaning to one's life and how this life really could be lived. However, a structured reflection and examination of beliefs, assumptions, characteristics and patterns can provide a better understanding which can lead to a more satisfying life and career. A greater level of self-understanding about important life skills is often necessary to make positive, self-directed changes in the negative patterns that keep repeating throughout life. The assessments and exercises in this book can help promote this self-understanding. Through involvement in the in-depth activities, the participant claims ownership in the development of positive patterns.

Journaling is an extremely powerful tool for enhancing self-discovery, learning, transcending traditional problems, breaking ineffective life and career habits, and helping people to heal from psychological traumas of the past. From a physical point of view, writing reduces stress and lowers muscle tension, blood pressure and heart rate levels. Psychologically, writing reduces feelings of sadness, depression and general anxiety, and leads to a greater level of life satisfaction and optimism. Behaviorally, writing leads to enhanced social skills, emotional intelligence and creativity.

By combining reflective assessment and journaling, your participants will engage in a powerful method for helping teens make more effective life choices.

Thanks to the following professionals whose input in this book has been invaluable!

Amy Brodsky, LISW-S

Carol Butler, MS Ed, RN, C

Annette Damien, MS, PPS

Kathy Khalsa, MAJS, OTR/L

Beth Jennings, CTEC Counselor

Hannah Lavoie

Jay Leutenberg

Kathy Liptak, Ed.D.

Eileen Regen, M.Ed., CJE

Special Thanks to Carol Butler, MS Ed, RN, C, for creating the Enrichment Activities

Introduction for the Participant

The teen years are exciting! You are becoming more mature and more independent each year, and you are now able to do new things that you could not do years ago. However, with this new independence also comes greater risk, and with this risk comes greater responsibility in the choices you make. It is critical that you become aware of the various risks that are inherent in society and understand that you have the power to ensure your own safety and that of your friends.

It's sometimes hard for parents or guardians to talk to you about safety, but your safety is their number one priority. However, as you become more independent, you need to take on more responsibility for your own safety in school and in your community, at your work or volunteer place, with your friends, at home and when you are online.

It is time to develop your own safety plan which will include your being aware of the dangers around you.

Some of the areas in which you need to worry about your personal safety:

- Risks related to violence including bullying, exposure to gangs, and harm from guns and other weapons.
- Online dangers including harassment, cyber-bullying, sexually explicit materials, identity theft and financial theft and scams, and agreeing to meet strangers in person after developing online relationships.
- Victimization of crimes.
- Risks while driving in dangerous ways, including driving after drinking or taking drugs, underestimating dangerous road situations, texting or using cell phones inappropriately and not wearing seat belts.
- Putting themselves in personal danger by pressures to do things they do not want to do such as experimenting with drugs and alcohol, having unprotected sex, going to unsafe places by themselves and engaging in risky behaviors.

The *Teen Safety Workbook* is designed to help you learn more about the dangers and risks in your life, and develop ways of coping with these dangers and risks.

CONFIDENTIALITY

You will be asked to respond to assessments and exercises, and to journal about some experiences in your life. Everyone has the right to confidentiality, and you need to honor the right of everyone's privacy. Think about it this way – you would not want someone writing things about you that other people could read. Your friends feel this way also.

In order to maintain the confidentiality of your friends, assign people code names based on things you know about them. For example, a friend named Sherry who loves to wear purple might be coded as *SWP* (Sherry Wears Purple). **Do not use any person's actual name when you are listing people – use only name codes.**

Teen Safety Workbook
TABLE OF CONTENTS

TABLE OF CONTENTS

TABLE OF CONTENTS

SECTION I:
Positive Feelings Scale

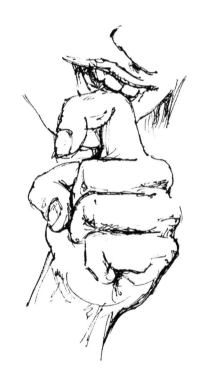

Name_____

Date_____

Positive Feelings Scale Directions

Everyone experiences negative feelings from time to time. These negative feelings often include stress, anger, low self-esteem, and depression. However, when these feelings become persistent in your life, it is time to explore, journal about and even express these feelings before they build up.

The Positive (healthy) Feelings Scale is designed to help you explore the negative (unhealthy) feelings that you may be experiencing.

Read each of the statements that follow and decide how much the statement describes you. Then, circle the number of your response on the line to the right of each statement.

In the following example, the circled number 2 indicates that the statement is **Somewhat True** for the person completing the assessment:

3 = Very True   2 = Somewhat True   1 = Not True

I.

I have a strong urge to run away from my life.................... 3   ②   1

This is not a test and there are no right or wrong answers. Do not spend too much time thinking about your answers. Your initial response will be most true for you.
Be sure to respond to every statement.

(Turn to the next page and begin)

Positive Feelings Scale

3 = Very True   2 = Somewhat True   1 = Not True

I.

I have a strong urge to run away from my life 3   2   1

I find it difficult to focus 3   2   1

I feel anxious a great deal of time 3   2   1

I often can feel my heart racing 3   2   1

I am eating and/or sleeping differently than usual 3   2   1

I feel a lot of pressure in my life 3   2   1

I - TOTAL = _____

II.

I find myself losing my temper and yelling 3   2   1

I am irritable and critical of others 3   2   1

I become angry when things do not go my way 3   2   1

I snap at people for no reason 3   2   1

I become angry instantaneously 3   2   1

I say hateful things that I don't really mean to other people 3   2   1

II - TOTAL = _____

(Continued on the next page)

Healthy Feelings Scale

3 = Very True   2 = Somewhat True   1 = Not True

III.

I feel like I am not good enough	3	2	1
I allow others to invade my time and space	3	2	1
I am unable/afraid to express my feelings	3	2	1
I often feel like bad things only happen to me	3	2	1
I blame others for my situation	3	2	1
I have a hard time trusting other people	3	2	1

III - TOTAL = _____

IV.

I have lost interest in all activities	3	2	1
I often see my life as hopeless	3	2	1
I often feel like I don't care anymore	3	2	1
I have withdrawn from others lately	3	2	1
I feel sad a lot of the time	3	2	1
I am constantly tired	3	2	1

IV = _____

(Go to the Scoring Directions on the next page)

Positive Feelings Scale
Scoring Directions

Exploring and dealing with negative feelings in a positive, healthy manner is critical.

To determine your feelings in each of the four sections, add the numbers you have circled for each of the four sections you just completed. You will get a number from 6 to 18. Put that total on the line marked TOTAL at the end of each section. Then, transfer your totals to the spaces below:

I	=	**Stress** _____
II	=	**Anger** _____
III	=	**Low Self-Esteem** _____
IV	=	**Sadness** _____

Profile Interpretation

Individual Scales Scores	Result	Indications
15 to 18	high	Scores from 15 to 18 on any single scale indicates that you currently experiencing intense, unhealthy feelings in this area.
10 to 14	moderate	Scores from 10 to 14 on any single scale indicates that you currently experiencing some intense, unhealthy feelings in this area.
6 to 9	low	Scores from 6 to 9 on any single scale indicates that you are not experiencing many intense, unhealthy feelings in this area.

You will find scale descriptions on the page that follows. Then, complete the exercises that are included. No matter how you scored, low, moderate or high, **you will benefit from every one of these exercises**.

In the following exercises, remember to use Name Codes for the people you describe.

Positive, Healthy Feelings Scale Descriptions

Following are descriptions of the four scales included on the assessment. If you are feeling very sad, depressed, angry or fearful, consult a medical professional or trusted adult.

Stress

People scoring moderate or high on this scale are experiencing unhealthy feelings related to all of the stress in their life. They feel pressure from bodily changes, outside sources (school, work, after-school activities, family, friends, bullying, violence, death of loved ones) and inside themselves (pressure to do well in school, pressure to fit in with peers, and pressure to make good career decisions). They feel anxiety and tension, become upset easily, and worry a lot.

Anger

People scoring moderate or high on this scale feel frustration and confusion that leads to feelings of anger. They are probably having trouble realizing their ability to control their angry feelings, and they are unable to express their feelings in a constructive manner. They may be experiencing trouble in school, at work, or in relationships due to their angry outbursts.

Low Self-Esteem

People scoring moderate or high on this scale do not feel good about themselves; they feel inadequate, unworthy, unlovable, and/or incompetent. They feel they are not good enough or do not measure up in some way. Thinking that leads to low self-esteem can be tied to personal looks, performance in school, adequacy in relationships with peers, performance in sports and other extracurricular activities, and relationships with family members.

Sadness

People scoring moderate or high on this scale are consistently sad for no apparent reason and often find themselves facing more than they can handle for long periods of time. They often feel lonely, agitated, uninterested about activities or people in their lives, and they are tired a lot of the time. They may also be experiencing changes in appetite, a lack of sleep or the need to sleep a lot of the time, and physical problems such as headaches. Sadness can lead to depression if left unchecked.

The following sections contain exercises to help you manage unhealthy feelings. Regardless of your scores on the assessment, these exercises will help you to feel better about yourself and feel more in control of your life.

What Stresses Me Out?

What types of things stress you out? Identify how you are experiencing stress and how you are dealing with it, either in a good or not-so-good way. Use name codes.

Areas of My Life When, Where, with Whom	How I Am Experiencing This Stress	How I Am Dealing with It – Good or Not-So-Good
Ex: School - SKZ keeps telling me she wants me to smoke with her.	*I get a stomach ache every time I see her coming.*	*I haven't had the courage to say no. I just avoid her.*
School		
Family		
Peers / Friends		
Bullying		
Career/Work		
Pressure to fit in		
Pressure to do well		
Changes in my body		
Other		

Stress can drive us to try our best or prevent us from taking appropriate actions. We need to be able to identify whether our stress reactions are having a positive or negative affect on us. It is important to recognize the ways our stress reactions direct our actions so that we can build on our strong positive reactions, but learn to re-direct negative stress reactions.

Tips for Dealing with Stress

Following are some activities you can do to reduce stress. Check the box in front of the items that you already do. The ones that remain are also good ways to manage stress – give them a try!

❏ Be realistic.

❏ Do not commit yourself to too many activities or take on activities in which you do not want to participate.

❏ Do not try to be perfect.

❏ Eat well-balanced meals regularly, cutting down on fast foods and sugars.

❏ Get enough hours of sleep each night.

❏ Play sports or exercise regularly.

❏ Remember that your attitude and thoughts can influence the way you look at things happening around you. Try to be as optimistic and positive as possible.

❏ Set realistic goals for yourself.

❏ Set small steps for large projects.

❏ Speak with a clergy member, religious or spiritual leader.

❏ Take control of what you can control and let the rest go.

❏ Take deep breaths along with positive thoughts
(I can speak easily in front of large groups . . .)

❏ Take time for hobbies and extra-curricular activities you enjoy.

❏ Talk to trusted friends, family, instructors or school counselors, to share your feelings.

❏ Think about change as a normal part of your life.

❏ Try not to compare yourself to friends or siblings.

❏ Try relaxing your muscles beginning down at your feet and relaxing all of the muscles in your body.

What Angers Me?

What do you get angry about? Identify why you become angry and then discuss how you deal with it. Use name code.

Areas of My Life	Why I Become Angry	How I am Dealing with the Anger
EX: Pressure to do well	*My parents expect me to get all A's like my sister.*	*I'm trying the best I can. I try to explain that to my parents.*
Pressure to do well		
School		
Family		
Peers / Friends		
Bullying		
Career/Work		
Pressure to fit in		
Changes in my body		
Other		

Tips for Dealing with Anger

Following are some activities you can do to manage anger in your life. Place a check mark in the box in front of the items that you currently do. The ones that remain are also good ways to manage anger – give them a try!

❑ Adjust your expectations of other people and situations (don't expect your friends to be as good at video games as you are).

❑ Avoid global attributions such as "This always happens to me" or "I'm the only one this happens to."

❑ Be assertive without being aggressive.

❑ Change negative self-talk patterns into more positive messages ("He irritates me when he acts that way" can be changed to "He's doing the best he can so I'll cut him some slack.")

❑ Count to ten before saying anything. This gives you time for your anger to subside.

❑ Know who and what trigger your angry feelings.

❑ People often get angry when they do not manage their time well.

❑ Play sports or exercise regularly to de-stress your mind and body.

❑ Step back and think before you speak – you will have time to change your mind.

❑ Take a deep breath and step back from the situation.

❑ Take time out and go for a walk.

❑ Try putting yourself in the other person's shoes.

❑ Try relaxing your muscles beginning down at your feet and relaxing all of the muscles in your body.

❑ Use humor to release tension.

❑ Visualize something relaxing (I'm at the beach, lying on the sand.)

❑ When possible, respond rather than react to a situation.

Low Self-Esteem

Identify why you do not feel good about yourself and discuss what you are doing about it. Use name codes.

Areas of My Life	Why I Don't Feel Good About Myself	What Can I Do About It?
EX: Family	I am impatient with MOG who lives with us. She's sick and always needs my help	I need to put myself in her shoes and think how I would feel if I were her.
Family		
School		
Peers		
Bullying		
Career/Work		
Pressure to fit in		
Pressure to do well		
Changes in my body		
Other		

Tips for Dealing with Low Self-Esteem

Following are some activities that can help you increase your self-esteem. Place a check mark in the box in front of the items that you currently do. The ones that remain are also good ways to feel better about yourself – give them a try!

❑ Accept yourself as you are.

❑ Allow yourself to be proud of your achievements.

❑ Be aware that being absolutely perfect is an unrealistic goal.

❑ Do not feel like a victim – take control of your own life.

❑ Don't commit to too many activities or activities you do not want to participate in.

❑ Don't give in to peer pressure to simply feel better about yourself
(ex., bully others to feel better yourself).

❑ Identify your strengths and weaknesses – we all have them.

❑ If it is reasonable (and healthy) change your looks
(wear your hair differently, lose or gain a few pounds, etc.).

❑ Make a list of ten things that others admire or appreciate about you.

❑ Make a list of ten things you admire or appreciate about yourself.

❑ Make friends by joining clubs, organizations, sports teams, etc.,
or volunteer for a local charity, but remember not to get over-involved.

❑ Realize that when you make a mistake it is not a reflection of you or
your self-worth.

❑ Set realistic goals for yourself.

❑ Skim through magazines and develop a collage by clipping out words and pictures
that represent your life.

❑ Take control of what you can do something about – and let the rest go.

❑ Try not to compare yourself to others.

Sadness

What are you sad about? Identify the sadness you are experiencing and then discuss how you are dealing with these feelings, or if you're not. Use name codes.

Areas of My Life	How I Am Experiencing It	How I am Dealing With It, or Not
Ex: Bullying	*I am being bullied almost every day.*	*I feel desperate and I am afraid to tell anyone. I know I should, but I just can't.*
Bullying		
School		
Family		
Peers		
Career/Work		
Pressure to fit in		
Pressure to do well		
Changes in my body		
Other		

Tips for Dealing with Sadness

Following are some activities that can help you deal with sadness. Place a check mark in the box in front of the items that you currently do. The ones that remain are also good ways to feel better about you and your life – give them a try!

❑ Avoid blaming others for your current situation.

❑ Do not expect too much of yourself.

❑ Eat properly and have enough sleep.

❑ Seek professional help from a doctor or another medical professional.

❑ Seek support from trusted family members and friends.

❑ Set realistic goals for yourself.

❑ Spend time with family and friends. Being isolated can cause you to be sadder. Continue to engage in social activities of interest, sports, after-school clubs or community volunteering.

❑ Stay as active as possible. Exercise can help! This can be as simple as walking your dog, playing basketball, taking a walk or going for a bike ride.

❑ Talk with a trusted adult in your life.

Remember – it is natural to feel sad when dealing with certain events and life changes. When it lasts for a several weeks, or if you are unable to focus or concentrate, it is time for you to talk to a trusted adult who can help you find a medical professional.

To the Facilitator:

The following pages will help teen participants to be aware of warning signs when sadness can turn into depression, and when depression can turn into thoughts of suicide.

Use these pages as appropriate with the teens who need them.

Depression and Suicide

Symptoms of Depression

The following symptoms are normal from time to time and arise for a variety of reasons, but experiencing several or more for more than two or three weeks may indicate the presence of depression or another mental illness. Check the symptoms that you believe a friend is currently experiencing, or check those that you are currently experiencing.

If you are answering for a friend, what is the person's name code? _____

❏ I cry or feel like crying a lot

❏ I am sad

❏ I am getting lower grades in school

❏ I'm bored

❏ I feel alone

❏ I feel empty

❏ I don't have confidence in myself anymore

❏ I often feel scared, but I don't know why

❏ I often feel angry

❏ I feel guilty

❏ I can't concentrate

❏ I have a hard time remembering things

❏ I have a hard time making decisions

❏ I feel like I'm in a fog

❏ I'm very tired, no matter how much I sleep

❏ I'm frustrated with everything and everybody

❏ I don't have fun anymore

❏ I feel helpless

❏ I'm always getting into trouble

❏ I'm restless and jittery and can't sit still

❏ I feel anxious

❏ I feel disorganized, as if my head is spinning

❏ I feel self-conscious

❏ I feel that nobody cares about me

❏ I feel ugly

❏ I don't care about what I wear

❏ I'm too fat / thin / short / tall

❏ My body is not shapely enough or too shapely

❏ I'll never make the team / choir

❏ I am, or I feel like, hurting myself

❏ I don't feel like talking anymore – I have nothing to say

❏ I feel my life has no direction

❏ I am consuming alcohol/drugs regularly

❏ My whole body feels slowed down

❏ I don't want to go out with my friends anymore

❏ I don't worry about my personal hygiene or appearance anymore

❏ My heart sometimes pounds and I can't catch my breath

❏ Sometimes I feel like I'm losing it

❏ I feel "different" from everyone else

❏ I smile, but inside I'm miserable

❏ I feel that life isn't worth living

❏ I have a hard time falling asleep

❏ I wake up and can't get back to sleep

❏ I have no appetite

❏ My appetite has increased – I eat all the time

❏ My weight has increased or decreased

❏ I have thoughts of suicide

❏ I have headaches, stomach aches and/or neck aches

❏ My arms and legs hurt

❏ I feel nauseous and/or dizzy

❏ I can't think straight

❏ Sometimes my vision seems blurred or slow

❏ I'm clumsy and feel off-balance

❏ Everyone hates me

If you have checked off several, it is time for you to talk to a trusted adult who can help you find a medical professional for yourself, or for the friend you had in mind.

How Teens Can Help Someone Who Might be Depressed

Depression is an illness that involves the body, mood, and thoughts. It affects the way people eat and sleep, the way people feel about themselves, and the way people think about events and people in their daily environment.

Just as we may plan regular tune-ups for our cars or schedule annual physicals, our mental health needs to be checked as well. The stigma often associated with depressive illnesses can prevent people from asking for help.

For those of you who know someone who might be depressed or suicidal, your helping this person accept and find help is extremely important. The first step should be to inform a trusted adult. Remember, you cannot do it alone! That person being willing to talk about depression and suicidal thoughts with a friend, family member, or someone they know, even if it is uncomfortable or scary, is essential in that person's receiving help and possibly in preventing a suicide.

If you personally recognize yourself in the following handouts, reach out and talk with a trusted adult who can assist you in finding help.

Remember, suicide *permanently* ends a life because of a *temporary* problem.

- If a friend or acquaintance tells you about suicidal thoughts or plans, immediately tell someone in that person's family or yours, other adults, or call 911, the operator, the police, a suicide hotline, or whatever number your area uses for emergency assistance.

- Remember, it is better to break a confidence and save a life, than to keep a secret. Secrets kill!

- If you have suicidal thoughts, tell someone you know will help you: a family member, other adult, counselor, teacher, coach, spiritual advisor.

- If you trust no one, or if you know no one, then dial 911, the operator, the police, a suicide hotline, or whatever number your area uses for emergency assistance.

NATIONAL SUICIDE PREVENTION LIFELINE

1-800-273-8255

Risk Factors of Suicide

- Alcohol and other substance use disorders

- Barriers to accessing health care, especially mental health and substance abuse treatment

- Changes in relationships and/or losses of relationships

- Cultural and religious beliefs that glorify suicide

- Difficult times at home and/or school

- Easy access to effective ways to die by suicide

- Family history of suicide

- Feeling of hopelessness

- History of trauma or abuse

- Impulsive and/or aggressive behavior

- Influence of others who have died by suicide

- Job or financial problems

- Lack of social support

- Local events of suicide that spread a contagious influence

- Mental disorders, such as depression

- Personality changes

- Previous suicide attempt

- Ridicule and/or exclusion in response to a different religious belief, unique cultural dress or celebration, sexual preference or gender identity

- Sense of isolation or abandonment

- Shame associated with seeking help

- Trouble studying and/or trouble with grades in school

Warning Signs of Suicide

- Anger

- Anxious, nervous

- Feeling as if there is no way out

- Feeling as if there is nothing to live for

- Giving things away, especially prized possessions

- High risk-taking behavior

- Isolating oneself

- Little to no interest in school or school work

- Loss of interest in surroundings, activities and friends

- No sense of purpose or belonging

- Preoccupation with death

- Sense of seeming distant

- Substance use

- Suddenly happier, calmer

- Thinking or talking about suicide

- Unpredictable, sudden, baseless changes in mood

- Visiting or calling people one cares about but hasn't seen for a while

- Withdrawing from friends, family, schoolwork, sports and school, and social activities

Something to Think about

Write about why you think a person might want to consider suicide (a permanent solution) at a difficult time (temporary problem) in life?

_____

_____

_____

_____

_____

_____

_____

_____

_____

_____

What Can You Do?

If you, or people you know, are feeling depressed or suicidal, what can you do?

_____

_____

_____

_____

_____

_____

_____

_____

_____

Positive Feelings: Thought-changing suggestions for teens from families struggling with substance abuse

Option #1:

- Distribute slips of paper and direct teens to write anonymously about negative thoughts they have had, currently struggle with, or anticipate having, regarding stress, anger, esteem and sadness.

- Collect the folded slips of paper in a cup or bowl.

- Teens take turns reading the negative thought aloud, and then replacing it with a positive but realistic one.

Option #2:

- Provide the following examples on slips of paper by photocopying and cut out the boxes below, or write your own negative thoughts on slips of paper based on what your clients are experiencing.

- Participants take turns selecting a slip of paper.

- Teens take turns reading the negative thought aloud and replacing it with a positive but realistic one.

---

1. I can't handle the stress of balancing my schoolwork, my job, my family and friends.

---

2. I get so mad at my parents for treating me like a child I feel like running away.

---

3. I feel like a loser because I am not accepted by that clique of popular people.

---

4. I am so depressed I feel like giving up.

---

5. I am beginning to believe I am gay, and I fear disapproval from my family and friends.

(Continued on the next page)

Positive Feelings: Thought-changing suggestions for teens from families struggling with substance abuse
(Continued)

Listed below, according to their numbers, are possible responses to elicit if participants cannot refute the negative comments.

1. I *can* manage the stress by setting up a schedule with some time for myself, deciding how I might cut out some work hours or unnecessary activities, talking with my family about their unrealistic expectations, asking my friends to understand my needs/responsibilities, looking up stress management and time management techniques online, accepting what I cannot change, changing what I can, etc.

2. I *can* deal with my parents by sharing my feelings, listening to their concerns, setting up a plan with my parents to get more privileges as I prove I can handle responsibility, realizing their concerns are because they care, reaching compromises, talking to other adults in the family who may influence my parents, etc.

3. I *can* decide what the "popular" people think (or anyone else thinks) is none of my business, get new friends, appreciate my tried and true friends, be a better friend to appropriate/supportive peers, join a club or volunteer for an organization with like-minded people, attend a house of worship to meet prospective friends, evaluate the "popular" crowd and decide I really do not want to be with people who shun others, etc. I *can* improve my self-esteem by doing things that make *me* proud of myself such as working hard, treating people well, being honest and ethical, saying affirmations to myself, developing my unique abilities, finding and working toward fulfilling my purpose in this world.

4. I *can* decide to press forward despite problems, to see a doctor and/or therapist, to develop coping skills and spiritual strengths, to know that adversity makes me stronger, to be aware that many people including sports, entertainment and political celebrities have survived sadness, to change my thoughts from negative to positive, to journal or draw my emotions, to exercise, to find enjoyable diversions, etc.

5. I *can* discuss my feelings with a school counselor or therapist, to further define my identity and preferences. I can hope that true friends and loving family will accept me, I can find new non-judgmental friends, I can talk with a counselor or therapist who will help me tell my parents, I can find support groups for parents/family of gays and lesbians.

SECTION II:
Healthy Choices Scale

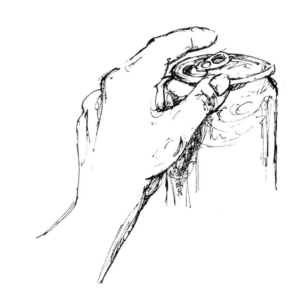

Name_____

Date_____

Healthy Choices Scale
Directions

Teens live in a complex world of multiple and often mixed messages. You are going to independently make a lot of decisions about how you want to live your life. You will be presented with many different choices and will be encouraged to do things you might not want to do. A responsible teen makes healthy lifestyle choices.

This assessment contains 28 statements divided into four areas in which teens need to make choices. Read each of the statements and decide whether or not the statement describes you. If the statement does describe you, circle the number under the YES column. If the statement does not describe you, circle the number under the NO column.

In the following example, the circled 1 indicates the belief statement is descriptive of the person completing the inventory.

SECTION I   YES   NO

I sometimes text while driving. . . . . (1)   2

This is not a test. Since there are no right or wrong answers, do not spend too much time thinking about your answers. Be sure to respond to every statement. Do not worry about totaling your scores at this point. Respond to all 28 statements.

(Turn to the next page and begin)

Healthy Choices Scale

SECTION I.	**YES**	**NO**
I sometimes text while driving.	1	2
While driving I usually follow the speed limit.	2	1
I am often distracted by talking on the cell phone while driving	1	2
I often forget to wear my seatbelt	1	2
I never drive after using drugs or alcohol	2	1
I often drive when I am sleepy.	1	2
I am a safe driver	2	1

I. TOTAL = _____

SECTION II.	**YES**	**NO**
I take drugs to reduce stress in my life	1	2
I use drugs to have fun	1	2
I have tried drugs out of curiosity	1	2
I have been pressured to use drugs, but said no	2	1
I use drugs because my friends do	1	2
I do not need drugs to fit in with my peers	2	1
I like to feel older by using drugs	1	2

II. TOTAL = _____

(Continued on the next page)

© 2012 WHOLE PERSON ASSOCIATES, 210 WEST MICHIGAN ST., DULUTH MN 55802-1908 ▪ 800-247-6789

Healthy Choices Scale *(Continued)*

SECTION III.

	YES	NO
I often drink alcohol to reduce stress in my life	1	2
I often binge drink (have more than 2 drinks at a time)	1	2
I have been pressured to drink alcohol, but said no	2	1
I drink alcohol because my friends do	1	2
I have tried alcohol out of curiosity	1	2
I do not want friends who will only accept me if I drink alcohol	2	1
I like to feel older by drinking alcohol	1	2

III. TOTAL = _____

SECTION IV.

	YES	NO
I stay in touch with someone I trust about my whereabouts	2	1
I avoid isolated places and try not to walk home alone	2	1
I often find myself in places where trouble is	1	2
I keep the doors and windows locked when I am home alone	2	1
I keep a cell phone handy so I can call for help	2	1
I am alert for trouble when walking alone	2	1
I travel in groups when possible	2	1

IV. TOTAL = _____

(Go to the Scoring Directions on the next page)

Healthy Choices Scale
Scoring Directions

This assessment is designed to measure how healthy your choices have been. For all of the sections on the previous pages, count the numbers of the answers you circled in each section. Put that total on the line marked "Total" at the end of each section.

Then, transfer your totals to the spaces below:

SECTION   I · TOTAL = _____   Driving

SECTION   II · TOTAL = _____   Drugs

SECTION   III · TOTAL = _____   Alcohol

SECTION   IV · TOTAL = _____   Personal Safety

Profile Interpretation

Individual Scales Scores	Result	Indications
7 to 11	low	You are not making healthy life choices.
12 to 13	moderate	You are making good healthy life choices sometimes, and sometimes not.
14	high	You are making very healthy life choices.

Following is a description of each of the four healthy choice areas measured on the assessment. Regardless of how you scored on the assessment, you will benefit from the activities and exercises that follow the descriptions.

(Go to the scale descriptions on the next page)

Healthy Choices Scale
Scale Descriptions

Driving Scale

Teens scoring high on this scale tend to demonstrate safety while driving. They tend to wear seat belts and stay within the posted speed limits. They do not drive after drinking or using drugs and they will not drive when they are sleepy. They are not texting or using a cell phone when driving since that is dangerous.

Drugs Scale

Teens scoring high on this scale tend to avoid the use of drugs when they feel stress in their lives. They do not need drugs to have fun and will not be pressured by peers to use drugs. They have not used drugs out of curiosity and do not use drugs to impress others or make themselves feel older.

Alcohol Scale

Teens scoring high on this scale tend to avoid using alcohol as a way of coping with stress. They do not binge drink nor do they drink to have fun. They do not feel pressured to drink simply because they want to fit in. They have never tried drinking to see what it feels like, nor have they used alcohol to impress other people.

Personal Safety Scale

Teens scoring high on this scale tend to keep trusted people informed of where they are and where they are going. They try to stay in groups and avoid walking places by themselves. They keep a cell phone on at all times and know who to call for help if they are in trouble. They make sure that they are safe at home.

Past Unsafe Choices

In the following table, list some of choices you made in the past that were unsafe, and then describe how these choices have affected your life so far.
Use name codes.

An unsafe choice I have made	How it affected my life
Ex: I tried alcohol with KUY as a way of being more popular.	Now KUY and his friends keep after me to drink more.

What patterns do you see?

_____

_____

_____

A Logical Decision-Making Process

The following is a logical decision-making process you can use when making safe choices in your life:

1. Identify the decision to be made. *(Ex: Should I give in and have sex with my LBF after the party).*

2. Identify the potential choices to be made. *(Ex: tell him that I am going to the party and not going to have sex afterwards; go to the party and have sex; don't go to the party at all, etc.).*

3. Identify and compare all of the possible consequences of the choices. *(EX: go to the party and have fun without having sex; go to the party and have sex even though I'm not ready and hate myself in the morning; stay home and do something else).*

4. Make a responsible decision based on all of the information you have available. *(Ex: go to the party and have fun but explain ahead of time to my boyfriend that I am not ready to have sex).*

5. Act on your decision and evaluate the results. *(Ex: went to the party, had fun, had a good time dancing, enjoyed myself without alcohol, and LBF didn't pressure me.)*

Your turn - Now you try it!

1. Identify an important choice you have coming up in the near future. What is that situation?

_____

_____

_____

_____

2. Identify the potential choices to be made.

_____

_____

_____

_____

(Continued on the next page)

A Logical Decision-Making Process *(Continued)*

3. Identify and compare all of the possible consequences of each of the choices.

_____

_____

_____

_____

4. Make a responsible decision based on all of the information you have available.

_____

_____

_____

_____

5. Now, think how you will act on your decision.

_____

_____

_____

_____

What do you anticipate the results to be?

_____

_____

_____

_____

Driving

Think about some ways that you make safe and unsafe choices while driving. Use name code.

While Driving I . . .	The Results of This Behavior . . .	How Could This Have Worked Out Another Way?
Ex: Texted BFF	*No problems*	*I almost got in an accident but swerved out of the way. It could have been deadly.*
Texted or talked on my cell phone		
Drink or use drugs		
Allow passengers to be rowdy or out-of-control		
Drive faster than I should		
Drive people I should not drive		
Drive an unsafe car		
Drive when I am tired or sleepy		
Other		

Drugs

Think about ways you make safe and unsafe choices related to taking drugs. Use name code.

Types of Drugs I Use Include . . .	The Results of This Drug Use . . .	How Could This Have Worked Out Another Way?
Ex: Tobacco Products	*I smoke and have no problems.*	*I need to sneak around. If my parents find out I'll be grounded forever.*
Cigarettes, etc.		
Marijuana		
Inhalants		
Depressants or Tranquilizers		
Stimulants		
Narcotics		
Hallucinogens		
Prescriptions or over-the-counter meds		

Alcohol

Think about ways that you make safe and unsafe choices while driving. Use name codes.

Reasons I have chosen not to drink ...

_____

_____

_____

_____

_____

_____

_____

Reasons I have chosen to drink ...

_____

_____

_____

_____

_____

_____

_____

Were there any repercussions for not drinking? Benefits?

_____

_____

_____

_____

_____

_____

How could some of your reasons to drink have backfired on you?

_____

_____

_____

_____

_____

_____

Personal Safety

Think about ways that you make safe and unsafe choices with your personal safety. Use name codes.

What I do to stay safe . . .	What I neglect to do to stay safe . . .

Staying Safe Pledge

I will do everything in my power to stay safe at home, school and work, with my peers, and in my community. This safety pledge is designed to help me stay safe and make safe choices.

When I feel I am at risk for any reason, I will talk to the following supportive people:

_____

_____

_____

_____

At Home

When I am at home alone, I will take the following precautions to stay safe:

_____

_____

_____

_____

I will confide in the following family members when I do not feel safe:

_____

_____

At School

When I am at school, I will take the following precautions to stay safe:

_____

_____

_____

_____

(Continued on next page)

Staying Safe Pledge

At School *(Continued)*

I will stay safe getting to school and returning from school by...

_____

_____

_____

When I am in school, I will talk with the following people when I do not feel safe:

_____

_____

_____

When I am in school, I will avoid the following types of peer pressure:

_____

_____

_____

In the Community

I will avoid the use of alcohol by...

_____

_____

_____

I will avoid the use of drugs by...

_____

_____

_____

_____   _____
SIGNED   DATE

Safe and Not Safe

Journal about the choices you make that ensure your safety.

_____

_____

_____

_____

_____

_____

_____

_____

_____

_____

Journal about the choices you make that may jeopardize your safety.

_____

_____

_____

_____

_____

_____

_____

_____

_____

_____

_____

A Safety Quotation

Charles M. Hayes wrote *"Safety First is Safety Always."*

Write three of your own thoughts about safety.

_____

_____

_____

_____

_____

_____

_____

_____

_____

_____

_____

_____

_____

_____

_____

_____

_____

_____

_____

_____

_____

_____

_____

_____

Warning Signs of Drug Abuse

- Aggressiveness

- Anxiety

- Change in relationships

- Depression

- Discipline problems at home and school

- Inability to pay attention

- Loss of interest in school, work, sports

- Mood swings

- Personality changes

- Poor coordination

- Reduction in memory

- Suddenly skipping school

- Trouble sleeping

- Withdrawing from friends or family

Facts about Drinking

- Drinking often leads teens to other drugs like heroin and cocaine.

- Each year, thousands of teens become permanently disabled or die from car crashes when someone in the car has been drinking.

- More than three times the number of teen girls who drink heavily report having attempted suicide.

- Teens who drink are more likely to engage in unprotected sex.

- Teens who drink heavily tend to complete fewer years of education that teens who do not.

- Teens who drink report having excessive anxiety and depression.

- The younger that teens are when they begin drinking, the more likely they are to become addicted to alcohol.

Healthy Choices: Decision-making suggestions for teens from families struggling with substance abuse

Option #1

- List these decision making steps on the board or large sheet of paper as a guide.

    1. Identify the decision to be made.

    2. Identify the potential choices to be made.

    3. Identify and compare all of the possible consequences of the choices.

    4. Make a responsible decision based on all of the information you have available.

    5. Act on the decision and evaluate the results.

- Distribute slips of paper and direct teens to write anonymously about decision making situations they face or may face in the near future regarding driving, drugs, alcohol and personal safety.

- Collect the folded slips of paper in a cup or bowl.

- Teens take turns reading a situation and making a decision based on the steps above.

Option #2

- List the decision making steps on the board or on a large piece of paper as a guide.

    See the above 5 steps in Option #1.

- Provide the situations on the following page by photocopying and cut out the boxes, or write your own situations on slips of paper based on decisions your clients may need to make.

- Participants take turns selecting a slip of paper.

- Teens take turns reading the situation aloud and practicing the decision making steps.

- Peers provide assistance and feedback.

(Continued on the next page)

Healthy Choices: Decision-making suggestions for teens from families struggling with substance abuse *(Continued)*

1. You are driving with friends in the car. The music is playing full blast, and they are talking and laughing. You would be unable to hear a siren and the noise is distracting you.

2. You just had an argument with your boyfriend or girlfriend. You are driving home and your cell phone rings. You hope it is your boyfriend or girlfriend calling to apologize. If you do not answer, the caller probably will not leave a message.

3. You are driving friends to a party. You tell them to buckle up and they do. Then when you are on the road, one friend takes off the seat belt and refuses to re-buckle.

4. You are at a party where everyone is using drugs. They encourage you to "just try a little bit, you will have a better time."

5. You are on a date with a person you really like. The person is drinking and tells you, "I don't want a relationship with someone who does not drink."

6. You started drinking with friends and now you really crave alcohol, or seem to need it to have a good time or to just feel normal.

7. Your boyfriend or girlfriend drove you to an event and has been drinking. You do not have a driver's license and do not want to be driven home by someone who is under the influence. The driver says, "I will break up with you if you don't go in my car."

8. You are alone at a friend's house and your friend shows you a loaded gun.

9. You are 16 and very attracted to a 28-year-old at work. The person gives you a lot of attention and compliments. The person asks you to go out.

10. Your boyfriend or girlfriend's "ex" is threatening to harm you. Your boyfriend or girlfriend tells you, "Don't tell anyone about it. Just ignore it. Don't get anyone in trouble."

SECTION III:
Social Media Safety Scale

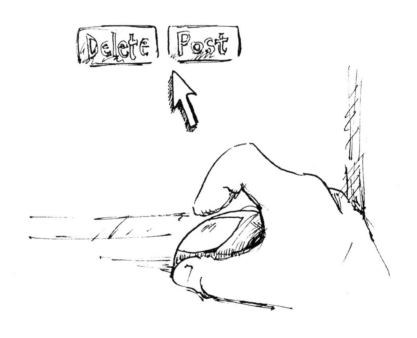

Name_____

Date_____

Social-Media Safety Scale
Directions

Cell phones, Internet and social-media sites have become tools which are appropriate when used effectively, but they can also put you in unsafe, dangerous situations. The Social-Media Safety Scale is designed to help you explore your safe-being when using technology.

Each scale contains 5 statements. Read each of the statements on the five scales and circle the number next to the statement that describes you.

In the following examples the circled 2 indicates that the statement occurs SOMETIMES for the person completing the scale.

	Always	Sometimes	Never
Chatting			
When chatting I use my actual name as my screen name 1		(2)	3

This is not a test and there are no right or wrong answers. Do not spend too much time thinking about your answers. Your initial response will likely be the most true for you. Be sure to respond to every statement.

(Turn to the next page and begin)

Social-Media Safety Scale

	Always	Sometimes	Never

Chatting

	Always	Sometimes	Never
When chatting I use my actual name as my screen name 1		2	3
I set up private chat rooms when possible. 3		2	1
I am not afraid to meet with online friends I don't know 3		2	1
I am cautious about people using false identities 3		2	1
I respond to all IM's even if they make me feel uncomfortable 1		2	3

I - TOTAL = _____

Social Media

	Always	Sometimes	Never
I often flirt with strangers online 1		2	3
I post personal information about myself on social media sites 1		2	3
I limit access of my pages to select groups of people 3		2	1
I post only information that I am comfortable with others seeing . . . 3		2	1
I feel safe giving personal information on blog posts 1		2	3

II - TOTAL = _____

Identity Theft

	Always	Sometimes	Never
I share my passwords with my friends 1		2	3
I do not store personal information online 3		2	1
I carry my social security card with me 1		2	3
I provide my credit card on unsecure websites 1		2	3
I keep my passwords secret, complicated and safe 3		2	1

III - TOTAL = _____

(Continued on the next page)

Social-Media Safety Scale

	Always	Sometimes	Never
Internet Surfing			
I never give out personal information on e-mails or websites	3	2	1
I illegally download music or videos	1	2	3
I visit sites I probably should not visit	1	2	3
I use updated versions of virus protection software.............	3	2	1
I visit sites that I know are not safe.........................	1	2	3

IV - TOTAL = _____

	Always	Sometimes	Never
Texting / Sexting			
I do not open or respond to texts of people I don't know..........	3	2	1
I text while driving	1	2	3
I make statements with texts that I would not make in person	1	2	3
I do not send or open explicit pictures	3	2	1
I have been bullied or harassed because of pictures posted or something I have said on a text	1	2	3

V - TOTAL = _____

(Go to the Scoring Directions on the next page)

Social-Media Safety Scale
Scoring Directions

With the advent of technology, social-media safety is critical for teens. For each of the five sections on the previous pages, total the number of answers you circled for each section. Put that total on the line marked TOTAL at the end of each section.

Transfer your totals to the spaces below:

  I = **Chatting TOTAL** = _____

  II = **Social Media TOTAL** = _____

  III = **Identity Theft TOTAL** = _____

  IV = **Internet Surfing TOTAL** = _____

  V = **Texting / Sexting TOTAL** = _____

Profile Interpretation

Individual Scales Scores	Result	Indications
Scores of 15	High	If you score high on any individual scale, you are **definitely** taking positive precautions to be safe while using that particular social media.
Scores of 14	Moderate	If you score moderate on any individual scale, you are taking **some** positive precautions to be safe while using that particular social media.
Scores from 5 to 13	Low	If you score low on any individual scale, you are **not** taking enough positive precautions to be safe while using that particular social media.

medium no media??

No matter how you scored, low, moderate or high, you will benefit from the following exercises.

Chatting

People scoring high tend to be sure of their safety when they are chatting online. They refuse meet people in person if they only know them from online chats, and they are careful about interacting with people who have identities that are unknown to them.

Ways I Am Safe when Chatting	Ways I Could Be Safer

Social Media

People scoring high on this scale tend to maintain as much privacy as possible in online social media sites. They limit access of information to people they trust, and they only post information they are comfortable having other people see.

Ways I Am Safe when Using Social Media	Ways I Could Be Safer

Identity Theft

People scoring high on this scale do not provide personal information online and do not use credit cards on unsecure websites. They use adequate password security for their social-media sites and do not give out their password to anyone.

Ways I Am Safe from Identity Theft	Ways I Could Be Safer

Internet Surfing

People scoring high on this scale tend to ensure their safety when surfing the Internet. They do not illegally download movies or music, and they do not visit sites they should not have access to. They also maintain adequate virus protection and security features on their computer.

Ways I Am Safe while Surfing	Ways I Could Be Safer

Texting and Sexting

People scoring high on this scale only text or respond to people they know and trust. They do not text while driving. They do not use the internet and their cell phone to send or receive sexually explicit photos.

Ways I Can Text Safely	Ways I Could Be Safer

Ways I Protect Myself from People Who Are Sexting	Ways I Could Be Safer

Benefits of the Information Highway

The huge variety of technology that is available to you has greatly benefitted your life. Think about how technology has benefitted you when you complete the following sentence starters.

The Internet has helped me _____

_____

_____

_____

My cell phone has helped me _____

_____

_____

_____

Social-media sites have helped me _____

_____

_____

_____

Texting has helped me _____

_____

_____

_____

E-mail has helped me _____

_____

_____

_____

Negatives of the Information Highway

The huge variety of technology that is available to you has probably also negatively affected your life. Think about how technology has negatively affected you when answering the following sentence starters.

The Internet has caused me_____

_____

_____

_____

My cell phone has caused me _____

_____

_____

_____

Social-media sites have caused me _____

_____

_____

_____

Texting has caused me _____

_____

_____

_____

E-mail has caused me_____

_____

_____

_____

Online Risks

The following are a few of the online risks associated with the use of social media and technology. For each one, describe ways that you, or someone you know, have gotten into trouble with technology. Use Name codes.

Risks with Social Media	What Happened?	How It Affected Me or Someone I Know
Exposure to inappropriate materials		
Downloading software		
Avoiding unsafe links		
Staying anonymous online		
Cyber-bullying		
Using mobile devices while driving		
Other		
Other		

Online Predators

The Internet allows anonymity rather than face-to-face interactions with people. People can hide their identity or even pretend to be someone they're not. Sometimes, this can present a real danger to teens online. Online predators may try to lure youngsters and teens into sexual conversations or even face-to-face meetings. Has this occurred to you or someone you know? Use name code.

Describe what happened.

_____

_____

_____

How did you, or the other person, handle the situation?

_____

_____

_____

What could you, or the other person, have done differently?

_____

_____

_____

Predators will sometimes send obscene material or request that teens send pictures of themselves. Have you had this occur to you, or anyone you know?

Describe what happened.

_____

_____

_____

_____

(Continued on the next page)

Online Predators *(Continued)*

How did you, or the other person, handle the situation?

_____

_____

_____

What could you, or the other person, have done differently?

_____

_____

_____

Sometimes, teens find a connection and begin to like online people whom they have never met. This makes them more likely to agree to a face-to-face meeting. Have you, or someone you know, had this occur?

Describe what happened.

_____

_____

_____

How did you, or the other person, handle the situation?

_____

_____

_____

What could you, or the other person, have done differently?

_____

_____

_____

Social-Media Safety

In your opinion, what is the intended purpose of social media?

_____

_____

_____

_____

_____

_____

_____

How do you use social media and technology safely?

_____

_____

_____

_____

_____

_____

_____

How could you be safer when using social media and technology?

_____

_____

_____

_____

_____

_____

_____

_____

Online Safety Quotations

At the end of the day, the goals are simple: safety and security.
~ Jodi Rell

Fear is the foundation of safety.
~ Tertullian

Journal your thoughts about either of the above quotations and how it applies to you.

_____

_____

_____

_____

_____

_____

_____

_____

_____

_____

_____

_____

_____

_____

_____

_____

_____

_____

_____

"I WILLs" for Staying Safe Online:

- I will allow my parents to monitor my social-media sites.

- I will be sure that my online profiles are as private as possible.

- I will change my user names and passwords often.

- I will not meet any online person that I do not know face-to-face.

- I will not share my password with friends.

  Your best friend today may not be your best friend tomorrow!

- I will report to an adult any abusive, threatening or harassing comments, posts or texts.

I Will NEVER ...

- I will never answer calls from unknown numbers.

- I will never download illegal movies or music.

- I will never forget to update my virus protection.

- I will never give out my password except to parents or guardians.

- I will never post personal information online.

- I will never send or display explicit photos of myself or anyone else on any type of social media.

- I will not do or say anything online that I would not do or say in person.

Social Media: Temptation suggestions for teens from families struggling with substance abuse

Option #1

- Distribute slips of paper and direct teens to write anonymously about temptations a person might have experienced with chatting, texting, social media, identity theft, surfing and sexting.

- Collect the folded slips of paper in a cup or bowl.

- Teens take turns reading aloud a temptation and sharing how they would respond.

Option #2

- Provide the following temptations by photocopying and cutting on the lines, or write your own temptations on slips of paper based on situations your clients are facing.

- Participants take turns selecting a slip of paper.

- Teens take turns reading aloud and sharing how they would handle the temptations, or pairs role play the tempting situations.

---

1. You meet someone your age in a chat room. You have many interests, likes and dislikes in common. The person wants to met you at a local park and "hang out."

---

2. Your friend begs to borrow your, or your parents' credit card for an online purchase. The person promises to pay you the money, with interest, within one month.

---

3. Your friends are gossiping on email and you have a lot of negative comments and juicy information you would like to share about the person(s) they are talking about.

---

4. Your boyfriend or girlfriend begs you to send photos of yourself in your underwear (or less) and promises, "The photos are for my eyes only. I'll never share them."

---

5. Your best friend wrote insulting lies about me on Facebook. You need to retaliate.

Social Media: Temptation suggestions for teens from families struggling with substance abuse *(Continued)*

Put the following roles on the board, and explain that children and teens from families where a parent abuses drugs and/or alcohol often follow at least one of these specific roles.

- **The Little Parent**

- **The Hero**

- **The Mascot**

- **The Chief Enabler**

- **The Scapegoat**

- **The Lost Child**

Ask participants to brainstorm qualities of each role, and write their descriptions on the board.

Following any of these roles may lead to unsafe and self-destructive behavior.

Use the information on the following page as guidelines, to elicit concepts they may have missed.

(Continued on the next page)

Social Media: Temptation suggestions for teens from families struggling with substance abuse *(Continued)*

- **The Little Parent** often takes care of younger siblings and may parent the addicted parent. They may be over-burdened by responsibilities and miss out on childhood/adolescent carefree times. Being overwhelmed may lead to unsafe behavior.

- **The Hero** is favored by parents, brings glory to the family by excelling in sports or scholastics. The Hero makes the family look good in the eyes of the world. They place high demands on themselves and think their worth comes from achievements. Parental demands, unrealistic expectations for themselves, and striving for perfectionism may lead to unsafe stress-relieving behavior.

- **The Mascot** is often seen as the Class Clown. The mascot uses humor to settle family disputes and make people feel better. The Mascot may be popular but is usually fearful of conflict and intimacy. Avoiding or inability to express feelings and lack of coping skills (except humor), may lead to unsafe behavior.

- **The Chief Enabler** is usually the spouse but may be a teen. The Chief Enabler covers for and helps the addicted person remain sick by lying or making excuses. They may pick boyfriends or girlfriends with substance abuse problems and tend to thrive on the chaos of addiction versus looking at their own problems, hopes and dreams. Seeking heroism by trying to save addicted or dysfunctional people may lead to unsafe relationships and behavior.

- **The Scapegoat** is labeled the Black Sheep or Problem Child and gets blamed for family pain/problems. Teens tired of being accused may stop trying to do well and play the bad role by fighting, bullying, getting poor grades, becoming alcoholics/addicts themselves. Negative labels or self-image lead to dangerous behavior.

- **The Lost Child** is ignored by the family or purposely hides out to avoid family pain. They don't get the material rewards or recognition the other kids get. They seek a life for themselves outside the family through friends, books, the internet/social media, video games, fantasy, television and films. Feeling lonely and outcast makes people vulnerable for unsafe situations, behavior and relationships.

(Continued on the next page)

Social Media: Temptation suggestions for teens from families struggling with substance abuse *(Continued)*

Ask teens to take turns identifying with one or more roles that they may play in their family.

Explain that the roles that help them function in a dysfunctional family may not be useful in the future. Encourage a discussion of how awareness of their roles will help break the cycle.

Ideas to elicit are listed below.

The Little Parent needs to limit the need have control or to be in charge; let go of responsibility for others and focus on fun and positive self-fulfillment.

The Hero needs to recognize that self-worth does not depend on making the family look good or on their idea of perfectionism. The hero needs to find personal interests and abilities, and know that personal best is good enough.

The Mascot needs to avoid over-using humor and to be in touch with their personal feelings and needs. The mascot needs not always to be the peacemaker; conflict is part of healthy relationships and conflict resolution instead of avoidance achieves results.

The Chief Enabler needs to know personal value is not dependent upon saving sick people. Chief enablers need self-actualization based on personal hopes and dreams.

The Family Scapegoat needs to get out of the troublemaker role. Being blamed by the family does not mean a person deserves blame. Family scapegoats can stand up for themselves, do their best, be productive and get recognition for doing right in the world.

The Lost Child needs to develop awareness of the tendency to run from relationships or to run toward any type of acceptance (no matter how questionable), even from damaging people or unsafe activities. The lost child needs to differentiate between healthy and unhealthy interactions and activities.

SECTION IV:
Relationship Safety Scale

Name_____

Date_____

Relationship Safety Scale
Directions

It is important to develop relationships in which you feel safe. Relationships can include friends, family, neighbors, employers, girlfriends, boyfriends and people in your community. It is important to explore your various relationships and examine how safe you feel in these relationships. The Relationship Safety Scale can help you identify the warning signs that might cause you to question your safety in your relationships.

In the following example, the circled 2 indicates that the statement is A LITTLE DESCRIPTIVE of the person completing the scale.

	SOMEWHAT DESCRIPTIVE	A LITTLE DESCRIPTIVE	NOT AT ALL DESCRIPTIVE
Someone I am dating ... Name Code L C R			
Makes all of the choices about what we do 1	(2)		3

This is not a test and there are no right or wrong answers. Do not spend too much time thinking about your answers. Your initial response will be the most true for you.
Be sure to respond to every statement.

(Turn to the next page and begin)

Relationship Safety Scale

	SOMEWHAT DESCRIPTIVE	A LITTLE DESCRIPTIVE	NOT AT ALL DESCRIPTIVE
Someone I am dating . . . Name Code _____			
Makes all of the choices about what we do 1	2	3	
Pressures me to have sex that I don't want to have 1	2	3	
Supports me and the decisions I make 3	2	1	
Does things that make me afraid 1	2	3	
Tells me the truth. 3	2	1	
Blames me for what happens. 1	2	3	
Loses temper often and scares me. 1	2	3	
Can be trusted 3	2	1	
Makes it easy to share my thoughts and feelings 3	2	1	
Swears at me or uses mean language 1	2	3	

A TOTAL = _____

	SOMEWHAT DESCRIPTIVE	A LITTLE DESCRIPTIVE	NOT AT ALL DESCRIPTIVE
Someone in my home or family . . . Name Code _____			
Makes choices and decisions for me 1	2	3	
Pressures me to do things I don't want to do 1	2	3	
Supports me and the decisions I make 3	2	1	
Does things that make me afraid 1	2	3	
Tells me the truth. 3	2	1	
Blames me for what happens. 1	2	3	
Loses temper often and scares me. 1	2	3	
Can be trusted 3	2	1	
Makes it easy to share my thoughts and feelings 3	2	1	
Swears at me or uses mean language 1	2	3	

B TOTAL = _____

(Continued on the next page)

Relationship Safety Scale *(Continued)*

	SOMEWHAT DESCRIPTIVE	A LITTLE DESCRIPTIVE	NOT AT ALL DESCRIPTIVE

A good friend . . .   Name Code _____

Makes all of the choices about what we do 1	2	3
Pressures me to do things I don't want to do 1	2	3
Supports me and the decisions I make 3	2	1
Does things that make me afraid 1	2	3
Tells me the truth. 3	2	1
Blames me for what happens. 1	2	3
Loses temper often and scares me. 1	2	3
Can be trusted 3	2	1
Makes it easy to share my thoughts and feelings 3	2	1
Swears at me or uses mean language 1	2	3

C TOTAL = _____

A neighbor, co-worker, supervisor or someone in my community . . .
Name Code _____

Makes choices and decisions for me 1	2	3
Pressures me to do things I don't want to do 1	2	3
Supports me and the decisions I make 3	2	1
Does things that make me afraid 1	2	3
Tells me the truth. 3	2	1
Blames me for whatever happens 1	2	3
Loses temper often and scares me. 1	2	3
Can be trusted 3	2	1
Makes it easy to share my thoughts and feelings 3	2	1
Swear at me or uses mean language 1	2	3

D TOTAL = _____

(Go to the Scoring Directions on the next page)

Relationship Safety Scale
Scoring Directions

The Relationship Safety Scale is designed to help you explore the safety of your interactions with particular people in your life. Fill in the code name of the person you had in mind when you completed each of the four scales. Add your scores within each section of this scale. Record each total in the space provided after each section.

A. Someone I Am Dating Total   Name Code _____   TOTAL _____

B. Someone in My Home or Family   Name Code _____   TOTAL _____

C. A Good Friend   Name Code_____   TOTAL _____

D. A Neighbor, Co-worker, Supervisor or Someone in My Community   Name Code _____   TOTAL _____

Profile Interpretation

Individual Scales Scores	Result	Indications
10 to 16	Low	You need to be seriously concerned about the safety of your interactions.
17 to 23	Moderate	You need to be somewhat concerned about the safety of your interactions.
24 to 30	High	You probably do not need to be concerned about the safety of your interactions.

Find the descriptions for the scales on the pages that follow. Then, read the description and complete the exercises that are included. No matter how you scored, low, moderate or high, you will benefit from all of these exercises by enhancing the safety in your relationships. Scale Descriptions are provided for the four scales you just completed.

Dating Relationship Safety – ALERT

People scoring low or moderate on this scale tend to experience the warning signs of a lack of safety in their dating relationships. This lack of safety may come from a girl or boyfriend pressuring one to do things the other doesn't want to do, losing their temper, doing things that cause a lack of trust, lying, and blaming the other for what happens in their relationship.

In the following table, identify your girl or boyfriends, past or present. Describe your relationship with each one and what about each one worries or scares you. **Use name codes.**

My Girl/Boyfriend (Past or Present)	How I Interact With This Person	Why I Worry About My Safety
Ex: SVH	We have dated several times and now he wants more from our relationship. I don't!	He pressures me and gets very angry and rough when I say no.

Who is a trusted person you can talk to about this problem?

_____

_____

_____

Dating Relationship Safety

Now that you have identified those people in your dating relationships who may be a threat to your personal safety, it is time to identify those people in your dating relationships whom you can trust and who do not pose a threat to your personal safety.

In the following table, identify your girl/boyfriends, past or present. Describe your relationship with each one and what about each one you can trust. **Use name codes.**

My Girl/Boyfriend (Past or Present)	How I Interact with This Person	Why I Trust This Person and Feel Safe
Ex: JRS	We go out every weekend.	JRS never gets upset with me if I don't want to do something he asks of me.

Review your list. What does this say about your choices?

_____

_____

_____

Relationships and Sexual Safety

Most of the time, when relationships begin, they are fun, healthy and exciting; they make you feel good about yourself and the other person. However, these relationships can turn unhealthy and become harmful to you. Following are some tips for developing and maintaining a relationship with sexual safety.

- **Share your feelings.**

    If you become upset or angry, talk to the other person about your feelings. Many assumptions occur in relationships because people are unwilling to share their wants, concerns and feelings.

- **Communicate honestly and openly about sex.**

    This will be the only way that your girl/boyfriend really knows what is comfortable for you – what is okay and what is not okay.

- **Know that you have the right to say "no."**

    You can say NO to sexual touching or sexual activity of any type in any and all of your relationships. If someone touches you without your permission, tell a trusted adult about the situation.

- **Understand that there is no such thing as "safe sex."**

    All sexual relationships come with risks – physical and emotional.

- **Touching other people sexually without their permission is not okay either.**

    You need to maintain appropriate boundaries in your relationships.

- **If you do engage in sexual activity, practice protected sex.**

    Protect yourself from sexually transmitted infections (STI). In a healthy relationship, you and your girl or boyfriend will protect each other's sexual health.

- **Remember that you can talk with a medical professional confidentially.**

    If you have questions about sexuality, protected sex or birth control – discuss it with a nurse or doctor.

Family/People-at-Home
Relationship Safety – ALERT

People scoring low or moderate on this scale tend to experience the warning signs of a lack of safety in their relationships with members of their family or anyone living in their home. This lack of safety may be caused by family members pressuring them to do things they don't want to do, losing their tempers, doing things that cause a lack of trust, lying, and blaming others for what happens in their relationship.

In the following table, identify your family members and/or people at home. Describe how you interact with each one, and what about each one worries or scares you. **Use name codes.**

My Family Members or People-at-Home	Why I Worry About My Safety When I Am Around this Person	What Can I Do?
EX: HNK	I don't trust her when we are alone because she loses her temper easily.	I can go to a friend's house as soon as I find myself about to be in the house alone with her.

Who is a trusted person you can talk to about this problem?

_____

_____

_____

Family/People-at-Home Relationship Safety

Now that you have identified those people in your family who may be a threat to your personal safety, it is time to identify those family members whom you can trust and who do not pose a threat to your personal safety.

In the following table, identify your family members or people who live with you. Describe your relationship with them and describe what about each one you can trust. **Use name codes.**

My Family Members or People-at-Home	Why I Trust This Person	How Do I Know I Can Trust This Person
Ex: GHY	We don't always get along but she never makes me feel like I'm not perfectly safe with her.	She always keeps her word.

Review your list. What does this say about your family and people at home?

_____

_____

_____

Friend Relationship Safety – ALERT

People scoring low or moderate on this scale tend to experience the warning signs of a lack of safety in their friendships. This lack of safety may come from friends pressuring them to do things they don't want to do, losing their tempers, doing things that cause a lack of trust, lying, and blaming them for what happens in their relationship.

In the following table, identify your friends. Describe how you interact with each one, and what about each one worries or scares you. **Use name codes.**

My Friends	How I Interact With This Person	Why I Worry About My Safety
Ex: LHG	Someone in one of my classes and my team, who lives close by and we walk to school together with other friends.	Is popular and bullies me into doing things I know I shouldn't – but I do it. I don't know how to stop – I don't want to be hurt.

Who is a trusted person you can talk to about this problem?

_____

_____

_____

Friend Relationship Safety

Now that you have identified those friends who may be a threat to your personal safety, identify those friends whom you can trust and who do not pose a threat to your personal safety.

In the following table, identify your friends. Describe your relationship with them, and what about them you can trust. **Use name codes.**

My Friends	How I Interact With This Person	Why I Trust This Person
Ex: SSB	She is in several of my classes and lives close by.	She and I have different likes and dislikes but she never pushes me to do anything she wants to do that I don't.

Review your list. What does this say about your choice of these friends?

_____

_____

_____

A Neighbor, Co-Worker, Supervisor or Someone in My Community Relationship Safety – ALERT

People scoring low or moderate on this scale tend to experience the warning signs of a lack of safety in their interactions with people. This lack of safety may come from people in their life pressuring them to do things they don't want to do, losing their tempers, doing things that cause a lack of trust, lying, and blaming others for what happens in their relationship.

In the following table, identify some of these people, describe how you interact with them, and what about them worries or scares you. **Use name codes.**

People in My Community, etc.	How I Interact With This Person	Why I Worry About My Safety Around This Person
Ex: SLJ	He is an older person who lives on my street and we say hello.	He seems to be staring at me all the time and is always outside when I go out! He follows me when I walk down the street.

Who is a trusted person you can talk to about this problem?

_____

_____

_____

A Neighbor, Co-Worker, Supervisor or Someone in My Community Relationship Safety

Now that you have identified those people in your community who may be a threat to your personal safety, it is time to identify those people whom you can trust and who do not pose a threat to your personal safety.

In the following table, identify people in your community, describe your relationship with them, and what about them you can trust. **Use name codes.**

People In My Community	How I Interact With This Person	Why I Trust This Person
Ex: SRD	I volunteer at a food kitchen and she works there.	When I tell her one of my problems she keeps my confidence and gives me good advice.

Review your list. What does this say about you?

_____

_____

_____

Problem-Solvers

Which adults can you trust, count on to be supportive to you, listen to your problems and give you good advice?

Possibilities	Name Code	Why This Person?
Teacher		
School counselor		
Principal		
Psychologist		
Parent		
Caregiver/Guardian		
Sibling		
Aunt/Uncle		
Grandparent		
Cousin		
Adult friend of family		
Friend's parent or grandparent		
Doctor		
Nurse		
Neighbor		
Co-worker/ Supervisor		
Clergy person		
Spiritual leader		
Other		

My Safe Relationships

Safe relationships are those in which both people display support, warmth and caring. List the people in your life with whom you have safe relationships. **Use Name Codes.**

Safe Relationship Characteristics	People Who Have These Characteristics (Use name codes)	How Do These People Apply Those Characteristics Towards You?
Honest & Trustworthy		
Support		
Tolerant		
Caring & Appreciative		
Respectful		

My Risky Relationships

Unsafe relationships are those in which one party lies and exerts pressure. List the people in your life with whom you have an unsafe relationship. **Use name codes.**

Unsafe Relationship Characteristics	People Who Have These Characteristics (Use name codes)	How Do These People Apply Those Characteristics Towards You?
Negative Peer Pressure		
Bully/Abuse		
Lie		
Fight		
Quick Temper		

Journaling about My Friends

Use name codes.

What is something unsafe that you don't you like to do, that your friends like to do?

_____

_____

_____

Which of your friends pressure you to do something risky and unsafe? (Use name codes.)

_____

_____

_____

Do you stand up to them? In what ways?

_____

_____

_____

If you don't stand up to them, how can you think about doing so? Who can support you?

_____

_____

_____

Do you pressure your friends to do anything they don't want to? In what ways?

_____

_____

_____

(Continued on the next page)

Journaling about My Friends *(Continued)*
Use name codes.

When your friends don't want to do something you want them to do, how do you listen to them and respect their wishes, just as you would want them to do with you?

_____

_____

_____

Some people have a toxic effect on their friends. In what ways do some of your friends use you?

_____

_____

_____

Which of your friends try to control you? How?

_____

_____

_____

Which of your friends want you to take unsafe risks? How do you react to them?

_____

_____

_____

Which of your friends gossip about you? How do you feel about that?

_____

_____

_____

It may be time to evaluate your choices of friends!

Journaling about Safety

"Safety never takes a holiday."

What does this quote mean to you?

_____

_____

_____

_____

_____

_____

What do you feel like you need to do to be safer?

_____

_____

_____

_____

_____

_____

What people do you need to be around and spend more time with, to be safer?

_____

_____

_____

_____

_____

_____

_____

Types of Abuse

- **Physical Abuse**
  is the act of a person touching your body in an unwanted or violent manner. This can include slapping, hitting, punching, kicking, pushing, biting, choking, or using a weapon against you.

- **Verbal/Emotional Abuse**
  is the act of a person saying or doing something that makes you afraid or feel bad about yourself. This can include name-calling, yelling at you, embarrassing you on purpose, blaming you, verbally pressuring you to do things you don't want to do, or keeping you from being with people you like.

- **Sexual Abuse**
  is the act of a person making sexual contact in any way you do not want. This can include a person threatening you to have sex, forcing you to have sex, or refusing to acknowledge unwanted touching or kissing.

A Safety Plan

- **Tell a trusted adult**
  parent, caregiver, grandparent, relative, school personnel, counselor, doctor, nurse, teacher, spiritual or religious leader.

- **Tell the person**
  how their behavior makes you feel. I feel _____ when you _____.

- **Avoid contact**
  with the person as much as possible.

- **Spend time**
  with people you trust.

- **Think about safe places**
  you can go in an emergency.

- **Call for help**
  if you need it.

Relationships: Role Play Suggestions for teens from families struggling with substance abuse

Option #1:

- Distribute slips of paper and direct teens to write anonymously about situations they have encountered, are dealing with, or may be confronted with, regarding dating, family, friends or members of their community.

- Collect the folded slips of paper in a cup or bowl.

- Direct teens to break into pairs with a person sitting next to them.

- The pairs take turns picking up a slip of paper, acting out the situation, making the safe decisions and taking the appropriate actions.

Option #2:

- Provide the following scenarios on slips of paper by photocopying and cut the boxes below, or write your own scenarios based on situations your teens are encountering.

- Participants break into pairs and select a scenario.

- They act out scenarios showing safe decisions/actions.

1. One dating partner pressures the other to have sex.

2. A friend encourages a friend to lie to parents about where they are going.

3. A supervisor pressures a worker to clock-out and work overtime without pay.

4. A coworker is observed stealing from the employer and tells the peer to keep it a secret.

5. An adult makes sexual remarks or advances to a teen.

106

SECTION V:
Self-Harm Scale

Name_____

Date_____

Self-Harm Scale
Directions

Self-harm are acts in which people deliberately inflict injury upon themselves. Self-harm is a type of coping device used when people believe that their emotional pain and suffering becomes too great to handle.

This scale will help you identify whether, and why, you use self-harm as a coping device in your life. Read each statement carefully. For each of the items, respond to each of the statements by circling the response which best describes you.

I do the following to myself . . .

1. I bite. . . . . Yes   No

In the above example, the circled YES indicates that the answer best describes the test taker's behavior.

This is not a test and there are no right or wrong answers. Do not spend too much time thinking about your answers. Your initial response will be the most true for you.
Be sure to respond to every statement.

(Turn to the next page and begin)

Self-Harm Scale

Respond to each of the statements by circling the response which best describes you.

PART I

I do the following to myself . . .

1. I bite	Yes	No
2. I burn	Yes	No
3. I cut	Yes	No
4. I bang my head	Yes	No
5. I pull my skin	Yes	No
6. I pull my hair out	Yes	No
7. I scratch excessively	Yes	No
8. I break my bones intentionally	Yes	No
9. I hit myself with an object	Yes	No
10. I stop my wounds from healing	Yes	No
11. I bruise myself	Yes	No
12. I have accidents on purpose	Yes	No
13. I punch a wall	Yes	No
14. I fall deliberately	Yes	No

TOTAL I = _____

(Continued on the next page)

Self-Harm Scale *(Continued)*

Respond to each of the statements by circling the response which best describes you.

PART II

I do the following to myself . . .

15. I swallow pills . . . . Yes   No

16. I starve myself . . . . Yes   No

17. I take drugs . . . . Yes   No

18. I drink alcohol excessively . . . . Yes   No

19. I swallow sharp objects . . . . Yes   No

20. I scald myself . . . . Yes   No

21. I stick sharp objects into my skin . . . . Yes   No

22. I swallow poisonous substances . . . . Yes   No

23. I drive too fast . . . . Yes   No

24. I pick at my body . . . . Yes   No

25. I throw my body against walls . . . . Yes   No

TOTAL II = _____

(Go to the Scoring Directions on the next page)

Self-Harm Scale
Scoring Directions

The scale you have just completed identifies various ways that people harm themselves.

It is designed to help you become aware of the possibility that you participate in self-harm behaviors. For both of the sections on the previous pages, count the number of YES answers you circled for each of the sections. Put that total on the line marked TOTAL at the end of each section.

Then, transfer your totals to the spaces below and add the two sections together to get your Grand Total score:

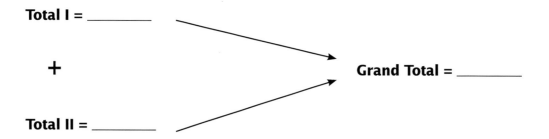

Total I = _____

+

Total II = _____

Grand Total = _____

After you have completed transferring your total scores, see the Profile Interpretation section below for more information about your scores on the scales.

Profile Interpretation

The following profile will help you learn the meaning of your scores.

Grand Total Scale Scores	Result	Indications
0	Low	If you responded honestly, you are not using any of the methods described to harm yourself.
1 to 25	Moderate to High	You are using at least one of the methods described to harm yourself. No matter how many methods you are using, whether it is one or more, it is not a good way to cope.

Regardless of your score on the scale, the following activities and exercises are designed to help you learn effective coping mechanisms.

What I Am Feeling

It is important to begin by exploring the feelings that you are dealing with when you harm yourself. On the worksheet below, write about the types of feelings you are experiencing. Use name codes if you are referring to anyone in particular.

Types Of Feelings	What I Feel
Ex: Hopelessness	*No matter what I do, I just can't get it right.*
Hopelessness	
Low self-esteem	
Anger	
Loneliness	
No control over my life	
Shame/ Embarrassment	
Guilt	
Other	

My Emotional Pain

Now it's time to explore the emotional pain you are currently experiencing in your life. Use name codes.

Areas of My Life	Emotional Pain I Am Experiencing
Ex: Family Life	*MGM and MGF are splitting up.*
Family Life	
School	
Changes in My Body	
Friends	
Work / Volunteering	
Dating Relationships/ Sexuality	
Other	
Other	

Why I Do It

Next, explore some of the potential reasons why you harm yourself. In the right-hand column describe some of the potential reasons you resort to self-harm as a coping mechanism. Respond to the sections that apply to you. Use name codes.

Potential Reasons For Self-Harm	Why I Do It
Ex: My feelings are too overwhelming	*It helps me to forget and hide what I am feeling*
My feelings are too overwhelming	
I want to escape reality	
I need to get relief from my pain	
I want to feel "real" again	
I must punish myself	
I am ashamed of myself and my actions	

Why I Do It *(Continued)*

Potential Reasons For Self-Harm	Why I Do It
I don't know a better way to deal with feelings	
I want to make the internal pain visible	
I can't express my feelings to anyone verbally	
I don't like my body	
I want to let others know there is a problem	
I'm addicted to hurting myself	
It makes me feel "alive"	
Other	

Looking For Patterns

Keeping a journal allows you to write about the worries and stressors in your life, as well as the overwhelming emotions that you are experiencing. By doing this, you will be able to identify the patterns that lead to self-harm and begin to deal with your emotions in a positive, non-harmful manner. Put a check by those worries and stressors that apply to you.

For the next week, on the next handout, write about your worries and/or stressors, to the point that you think about harming yourself. This will help you identify the stressors in your life.

Some examples of teen worries and stressors:

❑ abuse

❑ appearance

❑ being a bully

❑ being a spectator to bullying and feeling guilty

❑ being bullied

❑ dating

❑ depression

❑ divorce in a family (mine, family member, close friend)

❑ drugs and/or drinking (me, my family, family member, close friend)

❑ health (me, my family, family member, close friend)

❑ homework

❑ hunger

❑ lack of friends

❑ loneliness

❑ popularity

❑ poverty

❑ relationships

❑ school grades

❑ thoughts of suicide

❑ uncertainty of the future

❑ violence

❑ _____

❑ _____

❑ _____

❑ _____

❑ _____

(Continued on the next page)

Looking For Patterns *(Continued)*

Journal Entries	Name Code	My Worries and/or Stressors
Day 1		
Day 2		
Day 3		
Day 4		
Day 5		
Day 6		
Day 7		

(Continued on the next page)

Looking For Patterns *(Continued)*

After you have completed the week of documenting your worries and stressors, what patterns do you notice?

_____

_____

_____

_____

_____

_____

What situations seem to cause you the most stress and worry?

_____

_____

_____

_____

_____

_____

How can you recognize when you are nearing the point of harming yourself?

_____

_____

_____

_____

_____

_____

_____

How Can I Calm My Nervous Energy?

When you feel overwhelmed and out of control emotionally, try some of these techniques to manage stress and reduce your need to harm yourself.

Put a checkmark by those you are willing to try to do, or do more often.

❑ Adopt a hobby

❑ Avoid hot-button topics

❑ Avoid people who stress you out, if you can

❑ Be assertive – not passive, not passive-aggressive and not aggressive

❑ Be open to safe, healthy opportunities

❑ Be prepared and accept that unexpected problems will arise

❑ Breathe deeply

❑ Call a good, trusted friend

❑ Communicate your feelings, worries and stressors to trusted adults

❑ Consider ways to compromise

❑ Consider ways to forgive

❑ Dance, sing, draw - anything that you enjoy doing

❑ Do not try to control what cannot be controlled / Accept what I cannot control

❑ Eat nutritionally, without over-eating or under-eating

❑ Enjoy life's simple pleasure – smell the flowers, walk outside, etc.

❑ Focus on the positive

❑ Join a club

❑ Journal about your feelings associated with stress

❑ Keep a to-do list and work on reducing it

❑ Learn how to say "No" when it is appropriate

❑ Look at the big picture

❑ Manage your time

❑ Massage your neck

❑ Meditate or pray

❑ Plan your time

❑ Play sports, exercise or take a long walk

❑ Play with a pet

❑ Practice yoga, martial arts or other physical activities

❑ Punch a cushion to release anger

❑ Relax and listen to music that calms you

❑ Rip a magazine or newspaper

❑ Scribble, doodle, smear finger paint or use paint brush on paper

❑ Squeeze a stress ball

❑ Take a long warm shower or bath

❑ Take control of your personal environment

❑ Write

❑ _____

❑ _____

Using Up My Nervous Energy

It is important to identify non-harmful ways to use up anxious, nervous energy when you feel like harming yourself.

List the types of activities that help you feel relaxed and grounded, then what you enjoy doing and what you would consider doing. When you feel like hurting yourself, refer to this page for options. Use name codes.

Activity	I Enjoy . . .	I Would Consider . . .
Activities by myself		
Activities with my friends		
Activities with my family		
Activities that are creative		
Activities that are intellectual		
Activities that are physical		
Other		

PLAN
When You Think About Harming Yourself

One of the first steps in dealing with intense feelings is to talk with an adult you trust. Who are some people you can trust and talk to about your feelings? Use name codes.

_____

_____

_____

Share information with the person in a way that feels best to you. Remember that face-to-face is usually the most effective method for communicating. If you plan to use e-mail, snail mail, or some other form of communication, it would be eventually need to be followed-up with a face-to-face conversation. How will you communicate with someone from your above list?

_____

_____

_____

Express your feelings. When communicating with the person, focus on your feelings and what has led you to the point of harming yourself.

Practice by completing the sentence starters . . .

I am feeling . . .

_____

_____

The situation that led to these feelings . . .

_____

_____

Now I feel like . . .

_____

_____

Harming Myself Poem or Song

People who harm themselves are often unable to express their pain and intense emotions aloud. Try expressing yourself by writing a poem or song to express your pain. You do not need to be a poet or song-writer. This is just for you. If you wish you can use an existing piece of music and write your own words to it.

_____

_____

_____

_____

_____

_____

_____

_____

_____

_____

_____

_____

_____

_____

_____

_____

_____

_____

_____

_____

_____

_____

Draw, Scribble, Doodle

Draw a picture, scribble or doodle about the situation(s) triggering your intense feelings and emotional pain.

What I Learned About Myself

Based on the information and work in this chapter, what have you learned about yourself?

_____

_____

_____

_____

_____

_____

_____

What have you learned about your self-harmful behavior?

_____

_____

_____

_____

_____

_____

_____

If you find that your self-harming behavior continues, it is important to speak to a trusted adult to help you find a trained professional to help and support you:

- To develop additional strategies for coping
- To develop strategies for stopping self-harmful behavior
- To discover the root of the harmful behavior.

It is very important that people who harm themselves find someone they trust and one who has experience with self-harming behaviors. Your school counselor may be able to help or give you the names of professionals.

Why People Self-Harm

Some of the reasons people self-harm:

- Attain a "high" feeling
- Cope with overwhelming feelings
- Deal with feelings of separation and dissociation
- Ease tension
- Escape from emptiness and depression
- Escape numbness
- Feel a sense of control
- Feel alive
- Get attention
- Lack of support from family or friends
- Prevent suicide
- Provide relief when intense feelings build up
- Punish self
- Relieve anger
- Substitute expressing feelings
- Transfer emotional pain into physical pain
- Validate emotional pain

Environmental Pressures and Self-Harm

Some of the issues that can cause people to feel overwhelmed and out of control:

- Bullying
- Cultural difficulties
- Depression
- Discrimination
- Family members divorcing
- Feeling unpopular
- Feelings of rejection
- Gender identity / confusion
- Illness or accident
- Inability to 'keep up' with peers
- Lack of support from family or friends
- Loneliness or isolation
- Loss of loved ones
- Overwhelming responsibilities
- Physical or sexual abuse
- Poor body image
- Relationship problems
- Serious illness or addiction at home
- Suicide of someone close
- Unwanted pregnancy
- Worries about sexuality

Self-Harm: Interactive Suggestions for teens from families struggling with substance abuse

Option #1

- Distribute slips of paper and direct teens to write anonymously thoughts and/or situations that have or could lead to urges to harm themselves.

- Collect the folded slips of paper into a cup or bowl.

- Teens take turns reading aloud a thought or situation, and sharing a positive alternative to self harm.

Option #2

- Direct teens to brainstorm thoughts and situations that have or could lead to urges to harm themselves.

- A teen or the facilitator records them on board in front of the room.

- Teens take turns reading thoughts or situations and stating a positive alternative to self harm.

Option #3

- Break into two teams.

- Teams huddle in different corners of the room.

- Each team elects a recorder who writes their thoughts and situations that could lead to self harm urges on a piece of paper.

- Teams re-assemble in two rows of chairs facing each other.

- Recorders take turns reading aloud the thoughts and situations to the opposing team.

- Opposing team members take turns stating positive alternatives to self harm for the thoughts and situations.

(Continued on the next page)

Self-Harm: Interactive Suggestions for teens from families struggling with substance abuse *(Continued)*

Option #4

- Provide the following thoughts and situations by photocopying and cutting the boxes below, or write your own based on thoughts and situations your teens are experiencing.

- Participants take turns selecting a slip of paper.

- Teens take turns reading the thoughts or situations aloud and stating a positive alternative to self harm.

1. I feel extreme guilt over something I did or that was done to me. I believe I deserve punishment. Instead of self-harm I can . . .

2. I have no control over my life. My parents make every decision for me. They think I am incompetent. Instead of self-harm I can . . .

3. I want people to recognize how much I am suffering because I feel nobody loves me, people don't care. Instead of self-harm I can . . .

4. I hate myself. I feel fat and ugly. Instead of self-harm I can . . .

5. My boyfriend or girlfriend cheated on me and broke up with me. I'll never love anyone as much again. I'll never trust anyone again. Instead of self-harm I can . . .

(Continued on the next page)

Self-Harm: Interactive Suggestions for teens from families struggling with substance abuse (Continued)

Facilitator will try to elicit some of these alternatives to self-harm. (Alternatives are listed according to their numbers on prior page.)

1. I need to talk to a trusted person, a counselor/therapist/spiritual advisor about my guilt so that I can decide to forgive myself and the other person(s). I recognize that surviving this makes me stronger. I have learned from the experience and will not repeat the mistake or let myself be hurt again. I deserve healing, not punishment.

2. I do not gain positive control by harming myself. I gain positive control by doing what is best for me. I can try talking or writing a letter to my parents. I can negotiate ways to prove competence and gain trust. I can talk to a trusted person about ways to prove I can control my life. I can demonstrate maturity versus immaturity. I can gain control outside of my family by deciding ways to use my talents in sports, writing, drawing, helping others, working a part-time job, improving my grades, making my own decisions about my college/vocational school or career plans. I can join clubs, youth groups and organizations where I will be accepted as competent.

3. I can share my feelings by speaking, drawing, writing, crying, but need not harm myself to prove a point. I can decide to love myself and seek understanding and acceptance from positive people. Any of the following can help if available and appropriate: new friends, family, school counselors, doctors, therapists. I may find new friends by talking to classmates, joining school teams or organizations, joining a house of worship, helping a charitable organization.

4. I am thankful for the strong and useful body I have, and I can decide to change my diet and exercise plan or get advice about healthy eating and physical fitness. I can get help if I have acne. I can get a new haircut. I can develop attractive qualities such as being a good friend, never gossiping or bullying, helping others and working hard toward my goals.

5. I can decide the relationship was not healthy for me and I will be better off without the person who cheated or rejected me. I can choose to believe I will love and be loved again. I will hold a special place in my heart for this person and the good times we shared. I will also know what I do not want in future relationships. Trustworthiness will be a major requirement in a future mate. I will give myself time to heal before getting into another relationship. I will talk to prospective boyfriends or girlfriends to find out their views about commitment and honesty in relationships. I will recognize that possible break ups are a fact of life in any relationship, and I may have many on/off situations before I meet the right person for me.

wholeperson

Whole Person Associates is the leading publisher
of training resources for professionals who empower
people to create and maintain healthy lifestyles.
Our creative resources will help you work effectively with
your clients in the areas of stress management,
wellness promotion, mental health and life skills.

Please visit us at our web site: **www.wholeperson.com**.
You can check out our entire line of products,
place an order, request our print catalog, and
sign up for our monthly special notifications.

Whole Person Associates
210 W Michigan
Duluth MN 55802
800-247-6789

132